CW00498721

SERVICED ACCOMMODATION
WARTS AND ALL

How to Triumph over 14 Common Problems

in your Short-Term Rental Business

The ultimate guide to solving 14 of the most common problems in your

airbnb, short-term rental, or serviced accommodation business

ABOUT THE AUTHOR

Using the rent-to-rent model, Rae-Anne has scaled her business and built a property portfolio consisting of successfully managed serviced apartments, generating thousands of pounds for landlords in the private rental sector. Rae-Anne has managed hundreds of bookings across London and has been defining great, modern hosting since 2017 as the founder of www.yourserviced-space.co.uk.

DISCLAIMER

ACKNOWLEDGEMENTS

For Christopher, Isla and Mum, your support has carried me throughout.

Thank you for grounding me when times were tough, and for your continuous creative inspiration and love.

TABLE OF CONTENTS

INTRODUCTION

This book is the ultimate guide to overcoming the difficulties of owning a short-term rental or serviced accommodation business. You'll learn all the practical knowledge you'll need to make your property investment venture a success, including dealing with guests (demanding guests, guest scams, guest damage), business strategy (selecting cleaners, disputes with landlords, handling reviews), and payment and legal issues (chargebacks, payment merchant lockouts, security deposits).

This book outlines everything you need to know about running a successful serviced accommodation business from a property professional's perspective. Rae-Anne Rainford provides case studies and highlights mistakes to help you avoid common pitfalls and achieve your goals. Throughout this book, each section will introduce a problem (the wart) and offer potential solutions (the remedy).

SERVICED ACCOMMODATION: 'WART'S' ALL THE FUSS ABOUT?

Serviced accommodation (SA) refers to fully furnished accommodation that is made available for both short- and long-term stays. This includes houses, apartments, cottages and even individual rooms.

Compared to tenants in traditional rentals, guests that occupy serviced accommodation properties are given access to more space and hotel-like amenities and services. Examples of this include weekly housekeeping (cleaning and changing linen and towels), Wi-Fi, a fully fitted kitchen with top-of-the-line appliances and utensils, and electronic gadgets. However, not all serviced accommodation offers guest parking, and only some serviced accommodation offers things like on-site meeting rooms and fitness centres or gym facilities.

The serviced accommodation model offers more income potential than traditional long-term letting. This is why the industry has grown exponentially within the last few years, as individuals seek to take advantage of the increased revenue opportunities it offers. Serviced accommodation allows property owners to fill void periods, leverage off the higher holiday rates during peak seasons, and increase revenue by charging nightly rates.

The truth is that being a serviced accommodation business owner is a full-time job. SA is not a property strategy at all. It is a fully-fledged trading business and with it come the risks of business.

As a serviced accommodation business owner, you must now engage in operations, accounting, marketing, strategy, finance, personnel, I.T., and economics.

TERMINOLOGY

I understand that not every reader is aware of all the industry-specific expressions that are often used, so I will introduce some common phrases that will be used throughout the book, so readers can familiarise themselves with the terminology. Here are some good ones to start with:

- **90-Day Rule** – the prohibition on short letting a property for more than 90 days in a year

- **AST** – an 'assured shorthold tenancy'; a common agreement used by landlords to rent out residential properties to private tenants
- **BDC** – the abbreviation of Booking.com
- **Channel/Channel Manager** – the online distributor advertising or selling your inventory
- **Guest** – the paying customer who books, reserves or uses the accommodation
- **Host** – the serviced accommodation provider, operator, property manager, or property owner
- **No-Show** – the act of reserving accommodation but either failing to arrive or cancelling the booking
- **OTA** – the abbreviation of 'online travel agent'
- **PMS** – the abbreviation of 'property management software'
- **Remedy** – the solution or preventative measure to help resolve or treat a 'wart'
- **SA** – the abbreviation of 'serviced accommodation' or 'serviced apartment'

- **Wart**– a small, rough, and hard growth and, in this book, used in a figurative sense to describe problems in serviced accommodation

CHAPTER ONE
BUSINESS STRATEGY

1. BAD CLEANERS

The Wart

How long did it take you to find the ideal cleaning company for your serviced accommodation business? If you're new to the serviced accommodation industry and are still on your first cleaning company, be open to exploring other cleaning companies before settling on a housekeeping team.

I've personally been through six cleaning companies, and at the time of writing this book, I'm moving on to my seventh. That might sound overly picky, but issues like poor cleaning standards, poor attention to detail, failure to report damages, tardiness, and no-shows can affect my business negatively.

When you're still starting out, you'll likely want to find the cheapest cleaning solution so that you can cut down on costs, but this can potentially lead to major problems down the line. A housekeeping service is a key aspect of your SA business. Ask the following questions to make sure you choose the right cleaning service for your business.

The Remedy

Thoroughly Screen Potential Cleaning Companies – Things You Need to Ask About and Look Out for When Hiring a New Cleaning Company

- Does the cleaning company service any other SA operators?

If the cleaning company you're considering hasn't worked with other SA operators before, then you may have to do more work than you initially planned. If they already have SA experience, this means they'll likely be able to make your SA life easier.

- What systems does the cleaning company have in place?

Having a system in place makes managing bookings, cleaning schedules, changes, and notes much easier. Make sure the cleaning company you enlist is familiar with using a channel manager because this will simplify processes. I've seen people use spreadsheets and send emails for every booking – what a way to unnecessarily complicate things!

- Do they have any devices for communication?

Finding out what types of devices the cleaners and management use is key. Can they use these devices while on the go? This is a key part of communicating about general issues, new bookings, and other matters in a busy industry like serviced accommodation.

- What are their processes for tracking and solving issues?

Understand what the cleaning company's processes for tracking and solving issues are. This will help iron out queries before any problems arise. Find out whether they use WhatsApp group chats, email, calls, or other methods of communication.

- How do they handle check-ins and check-outs?

Is the housekeeping service able to facilitate early check-ins and check-outs? Ask them if they'll clean on the day of check-in and after every check-out. This will help you take stock of any damage and other issues in time so that you can charge the guest responsible.

This means you'll also be able to maximise revenue by facilitating same-day bookings in the OTA portal because you'll know that the properties will be ready for new guests. This will also help you identify guests who checked out late or didn't pay for over-occupancy. You'll be surprised at how much guests can do to pull the wool over your eyes. On one occasion, I caught 17 guests who had booked for six!

- How will linens be handled?

Will the cleaning company collect and wash purchased linens, or do they hire out linens? If they do it themselves, do they have a central office for linen storage, drop-offs, and collections? You should also consider whether they can deal with linen tickets that notify which linen needs to be taken away and collected. Last, knowing whether they can track linen counts is important because it'll help you monitor usage and costs.

- Will they be in charge of consumables?

Having a cleaning company that's able to order, hold, and replenish stock can save you a lot of time and money – even if you have to pay extra. As an added bonus, you'll be able to use the company's trade accounts to your advantage because they have better buying power.

- How will the keys be handled?

Central key storage for cleaners is important, so make sure the cleaning company offers this. You also want to consider how the keys are tagged. Should the keys get lost, they shouldn't be tagged with information that could lead someone to your unit.

- Are keyholding facilities included?

Keyholding services are important. Make sure the cleaning service can return keys to where they're meant to be, if a guest forgets to return them upon checking out. Keynest is a great solution for serviced accommodation.

- Can they facilitate meet-and-greets?

When you're new to serviced accommodation, you may feel the need to spend time meeting your guests because of your attachment to your new investment. After a while, you'll realise that you should spend your time elsewhere, as most guests just want to check in and see the accommodation. Make sure that the housekeeping company you hire can facilitate meet-and-greets if and when required.

- What areas do the cleaners cover, and are they mobile?

Knowing what areas a cleaning company covers and how mobile they are will help you choose the best one. Ideally, a cleaning company should cover where your serviced accommodation is located, and they should be able to get from point A to point B easily.

- What are the team's dynamics?

Working with a team of people requires you to know the team's strengths. This includes how many people are on the team, how many cleaners they use per turnover, and what their process is if cleaners are ill. Avoid cleaning companies where owners clean and manage simultaneously. It's a recipe for disaster, trust me!

- Do they offer spot-checking and inspections?

Finding out whether the cleaning company does spot-checking and inspections regularly is key. You never want your guests to notice issues before you. However, visiting your properties to look for issues yourself is time-consuming. Hiring a qualified property manager can help with this kind of duty.

- What levels of cleaning are available?

Contrary to popular belief, not all cleaning is equal. You should ask the cleaning company you're planning to hire what their cleaning services include. It's best to never assume! Some cleaning companies have the following levels of cleaning:

- Builder's clean
- Holiday rental clean
- End of tenancy clean
- Mid-stay clean (or top-up clean)
- Office clean
- Domestic clean
- What do they charge?

You'll have to factor the cost of hiring a cleaning company into your expenses. Bear in mind that a VAT-registered company will increase your costs significantly. You should also find out whether they charge on an hourly basis or offer a fixed per-turnover cost (which saves you money and prevents issues with tracking cleaning invoices).

Costs should ideally include services such as linen changes, cleaning, and consumable refreshes. Asking the cleaning company what they consider 'dirty' is important because one person's perception of cleanliness is different from another's. If you aren't clear on the company's offering, you might get billed extra for services you thought were standard.

- How do they handle invoicing?

How does the company invoice? Is it per calendar month and by apartment? This will make it easier to track costs.

- What is their payment policy?

A favourable payment term (such as 14 days) can help your business with cash flow. Find out what the cleaning company's payment policy is so that you can plan your finances accordingly.

• What are their future plans?

Is the cleaning company you're hiring willing to grow with you? You will only know this if you ask what their plans are for the future and see whether they match your business goals. Unfortunately, I've had to don the yellow gloves on odd occasions to deal with lazy cleaners or cleaning company owners who didn't know how to run their businesses properly.

I currently use five different self-employed cleaning companies that service 42 apartments. Even though I've had issues with these companies at various points, I've held meetings with them to discuss the importance of cleanliness and why they're paid £15 per hour. When attending the property, the cleaners use a checklist to mark off tasks, with photographs, in case they have missed something (like toilet paper, tea towels, or cleaning a spot properly), which minimises the number of complaints and increases guest satisfaction. Doing regular spot-checks on all the apartments also helps in this regard.

Apps like TurnoverBnB and Properly are excellent for streamlining and automating check-ins. These apps allow you to link each of your properties to an iCal link, which creates a new cleaning project for your cleaners to accept every time you receive a new booking. These property management apps also allow you to invite as many cleaners as you'd like to the app, and they will automatically update any bookings and cancellations from the channel manager.

- What happens if you give your cleaners too many tasks?

Ground operations is an expense that serviced accommodation owners should factor into their budget. Some owners prefer for their housekeepers to do these tasks for free to save money, but this can cause problems down the line, especially if the owner makes assumptions about the cleaning company's capabilities and costs. It's best to ask whether they can handle any extra tasks and whether this will lead to an increase in price. There will most likely be additional charges, but you can determine whether the charges are reasonable based on the amount you're paying in the first place.

Keep in mind that a cleaning service offers only cleaning, whereas a housekeeping service may include cleaning and other tasks. Most cleaning services are designed for regular or one-off domestic cleaning, and expecting them to conduct changeovers, meet-and-greets, laundry, weekends, and more for a basic cleaning fee is not realistic or sustainable.

There are more cleaning clients than companies, so it makes sense that no cleaning company will pivot their entire business model to accommodate you. Make sure you hire the right service for the job. The last thing you want is for things to go wrong because you've misunderstood the company's role in your serviced accommodation.

2. DOUBLE-BOOKINGS

The Wart

One of the worst things you can do as a serviced accommodation business owner is forgetting to block your availability. However, sometimes you're not making the mistake – the CM or OTA is. This has happened to me. The API between my CM and Airbnb went down, resulting in an accidental double-booking. Thankfully, I was able to get Airbnb to cancel the booking without penalty after proving what had happened.

There could be a myriad of reasons for double-bookings, but the solution is usually to reach out to the channel manager and ask them to investigate what caused it. The issue is usually on the channel manager's end rather than the OTA's.

The Remedy

The solution to double-bookings is finding a reliable channel manager. You can also use your competition and contact them in situations like this. Contacting the guest to explain the situation and offering to help them with relocation (if possible) is a great solution to double-booking.

Facebook groups for serviced accommodation owners in your area are also a great way to solve double-bookings and other issues. You can post there and ask if another local provider can offer the guest an upgrade. Be sure to include the area, dates, and number of guests – someone will respond if they have availability. I find that if you speak to the guest, they are more likely to understand and cancel their booking than if you just speak to the OTA.

3. BAD GUEST REVIEWS

The Wart

Now, there will undoubtedly come a time when a guest has something bad to say about you, your business, the accommodation, or the service that you provide. Unfortunately, this is human nature, and in this business, it is extremely difficult to please everyone. Sometimes, the guest rips you to shreds in their review for no fault of your own, and other times, you face retaliation reviews for their bad behaviour, a cancelled booking, or them simply breaking house rules. There are other instances where a guest leaves no comment at all, just a low score or rating. This will affect your overall listings performance, and if this is on BDC, you're usually unable to respond to a review with no comments. These are the most infuriating reviews in my opinion because having an opportunity to respond gives you the chance to turn things around, particularly if the guest simply had a bad experience in your property.

The Remedy

If you're on BDC, you'll be able to file a gross misconduct report against the guest, which will prevent them from leaving a review. You also have the opportunity to respond to the guest if they do leave a review with commentary, but you need to remember that you're not talking to that particular guest but rather to the potential guests who will be reading the review. Your anger and frustration when reading an unfair review are valid, but I suggest keeping your response calm and professional.

Reviews are important, but don't get too hung up on them. The quicker you learn to respond to them appropriately and move on, the better. As difficult as it may be, try not to see the review as a personal attack (even if it is) and never respond in a personal manner.

A potential recourse for bad reviews is to call or email the guest and ask if they made a mistake by reviewing the wrong place. If they made a mistake, they'll be able to remove the review on their end, and if not, you can use the opportunity to ask them about what you could've done as a host to receive a better rating. Overall, don't dwell on bad reviews. Some guests can't be pleased no matter what and will always leave a low score without a valid reason. It's not worth worrying over.

Here are some hacks for reviews left by guests on channels such as Booking.com and Airbnb. For BDC, you can mark the guest as a 'no-show'. This will prevent BDC from asking the guest to review their stay. BDC will contact the guest to confirm this once you've marked them as a no-show, but by then it won't matter.

For Airbnb, if the guest's review goes against their review policy, you can request that the review be removed from Airbnb entirely. Any content from a review about services unrelated to Airbnb, the guest's stay or experience, or circumstances outside of your control goes against Airbnb's review policy. I always recommend having a look at the full details of their review policy to familiarise yourself, but in summary, Airbnb states that a review should:

- not violate their content policy
- be unbiased
- be relevant

4. GLOBAL PANDEMICS (COVID-19)

The Wart

With hosts losing all calendar bookings, an increase in commission fees, and OTAs prioritising guests over hosts, the COVID-19 pandemic has shown us that SA operators cannot depend solely on OTAs for the future of their serviced accommodation businesses. The phrase 'don't build your house on someone else's land' is very important in this regard, but you can still take advantage of the huge marketing opportunity that OTAs offer and convert leads into direct bookings, which equal more money in your pocket than bookings through the OTA. To do this effectively, you need to ensure that your OTA listings are optimised to attract bookings.

The Remedy

Offer guests the option of booking directly with you for a discounted rate. This option will be attractive if you're offering a discount of at least 10%. It will incentivise them to cancel and book directly through you. Make it a win-win situation for all.

Using your company's logo and corporate identity in your marketing materials on the OTAs is also key because it tells potential guests who you are and how they can find you. However, you shouldn't be explicit about this because this can lead to the OTAs penalising you. An example of this type of covert marketing would be using your company logo as your profile picture on the OTA.

Email marketing is also an excellent way to convert bookings from the OTA to direct bookings. It's a form of marketing that every SA operator should be privy to, and if you don't have a mailing list of previous or potential guests, you're missing out! Start building your email list now. It's a powerful marketing tool that can increase your revenue. The best thing about an email list is that it's owned by you and nobody else, so you have full control over it – unlike social media and OTAs, which are owned by corporations that can ban or restrict your account according to their discretion. Email lists are also free, which makes the return on investment enormous if you're able to send your mailing list compelling one-off offers.

CHAPTER TWO
DEALING WITH GUESTS

5. DEMANDING GUESTS, PROPERTY MISHAPS, AND REFUND HUNTERS

The Wart

Sometimes a guest doesn't want to pay full price or doesn't want to pay at all, so they create or exaggerate flaws and failures in your product or service. This is where being 'nice' goes out the window. My company policy strictly states that we don't refund, *we rectify*. I never offer or pay compensation, thanks to my robust terms and policies.

The fact is, professional refund hunters exist. While the average person spends money on solo trips or group excursions to enjoy them, some people are hell-bent on having a terrible time and will do their best to pay little to nothing for the privilege. They are some of the most demanding individuals you'll ever encounter. Trips aren't always perfect, and a customer won't always be satisfied with your accommodation, but those aren't the types of individuals I'm discussing here. I'm talking about the types of individuals who usually start complaining right away!

The Remedy

I recommend only offering refunds in extenuating circumstances. The refund offered should be about 10% to 15% of the guest's total reservation cost (as recommended by Airbnb). Extenuating circumstances include no hot water or heating, a flooded room, and similar issues. In other instances, it isn't necessary to refund a guest because a solution to the problem can be found. On several occasions, I've offered to refund a guest a night of accommodation when I was unable to solve their issue during their reservation, but this doesn't happen very often. Now, I make sure I have a reliable team that's ready to deal with issues efficiently. Your team should ideally consist of housekeepers, handymen, property managers, and meet-and-greet clerks.

Top tip: Make sure you register with Amazon Prime to get items delivered to the guest the same day or the next day.

6. GUEST LOCKOUTS AND LOST KEYS

The Wart

This often happens at the most inconvenient time. Sometimes a guest locks themselves out, resulting in an unwanted emergency call at an ungodly hour. Other times, a guest loses a key and needs urgent help. Here's how you can handle these challenging situations.

The Remedy

You should always keep a spare set of keys (also known as cleaner's keys) in a lockbox or at a local shop. Using KeyNest to keep track of keys is also a great alternative. I've given my cleaner's set of keys to guests in an emergency like this, and it has been a lifesaver that prevented me or any other staff member from being called out at a late hour.

Sometimes guests will leave and not return the keys. For safety reasons, it's best to assume that lost keys are never actually lost. Should this happen to you, don't bother paying a locksmith. Instead, learn how to swap out a barrel yourself and keep the old one as a spare (just in case you need to swap it out again). All you need is the right barrel and a cross-eye screwdriver. You'll have to remove the plate on the edge of the door if there is one, undo the long screw that secures the barrel in the door, pop the barrel out, and slide the new one in. Then, secure the new barrel with the long screw and put the plate back. Voila!

Further Steps I Take to Deal with Guest Lockouts and Lost Keys

Consider keyless access via wireless door locks for your guests. Instead of needing traditional keys, guests can use a code to gain access to the apartment. If the property is in an apartment block or a gated community, they'll also need the code for the main entrance. I use the Klevio app for guest codes, which allows me to be completely keyless across all the properties I manage.

Going keyless will provide you more control, the ability to make the digital keys expire (which helps with guests who check out late), an easy means to grant and revoke access to the property, zero headaches resulting from lost keys, and increased security.

7. GUEST SCAMS

The Wart

I have been hosting for quite some time now and have seen my share of shady and suspicious guests. Some guests go out of their way to finagle you. There are three main types of guest scams:

1. The guest books an initial stay and pays upfront. During their stay, they ask if they can extend their booking. They then decide not to pay for the stay since they're already in the apartment. You may resort to calling the police on them, but they'll tell the police that they're a tenant, resulting in the police deeming it a 'civil matter' that can be solved by the two of you. If you don't have concrete evidence that proves that they are indeed a guest and not a tenant, you may have to approach the courts and legally repossess your property.

2. The second type of scam involves guests advertising your property online, renting it out to a tenant, and disappearing with their rent and their deposit.

This leaves you with a tenant with or without a fake AST. It may even leave you wondering whether the tenant is a part of the scam or not.

3. The third type of scam is the mail scam. It involves using an Airbnb property as proof of address for fraudulent activities like identity theft. Some guests order expensive items and have them shipped to the address. Others authenticate information to illegally obtain bank accounts and credit cards for money laundering, money mule accounts, and fake businesses. Their stories might sound convincing, but don't fall for it! Don't allow guests to mail anything to your property. The only exceptions are a long-term guest who is staying at the property or a return guest.

The Remedy

The best way to deal with guest scams is to educate yourself on the different types of scams (which is the purpose of this section of the book). You should also protect your business by knowing the difference between 'licence to stay' and tenancy. Before letting people into your property, make sure you're clear about whether they'll be guests or tenants. This will determine the type of paperwork you have to use. If they're using your apartment as a primary residence, they'll be tenants, and the paperwork has to be an AST. If they don't satisfy both of the AST tests, then they'll be considered guests, and you can use a licence.

If guests end up advertising your property online and renting it out, keep in mind that the guest's 'tenants' have no rights because the AST was issued by an unauthorised party. They will have to contact the police, who will likely refer them to Action Fraud because they are the ones who suffered the loss. You'll have to evict the tenant from the property right away and may even find that the original guest's booking was paid for using a stolen credit card, so anticipate chargeback fees (see point number 2). For this reason, you should have a booking form with terms that explicitly state that guests have no rights under the Housing Act. For example, you can add a clause similar to this:

> *Security of Tenure: All the apartments are occupied as serviced apartments, and on this basis, no rights of tenancy are created. Therefore, they are exempt from security of tenure under the Rent Act. My Serviced Space reserves the right to access the apartment and/or terminate your stay at any time without prior notice if it deems necessary.*

You should also consider adding terms stating in your house rules and guest message templates that you don't accept mail. I say something along the lines of 'we advise against using the property address to receive mail or post, as we do not have access to the mailboxes.'

Direct guests who want their deliveries to come to the apartment to an Amazon locker instead. Amazon ships to locations and establishments with Amazon lockers, and all a guest needs is ID and a credit card. Should they need a temporary address, you can offer them a web link with the address of a courier post office. It's the perfect solution for guests who are staying in the short term.

The key is to also ensure that the guest has a main residence elsewhere. For longer stays, make sure you continue servicing the apartment by sending in your cleaner weekly. This allows you to stay in direct control of what happens to your apartment, offer guests the serviced accommodation they're paying for, and make sure that they don't have exclusive possession of it. Never fall for 'Oh, it's okay; we'll do the cleaning.'

8. GUEST DAMAGE OR THEFT

The Wart

You may have spent a lot of time and money decorating the place before making it available for short-term letting. You've may have repainted, invested in top-of-the-line electrical appliances, laid new carpet, or put up artwork. All this effort can go down the drain if you deal with a guest who damages or steals your property.

Lost keys, stolen furniture, broken door handles, and trashed valuables are common issues when hosting your property as a short-term rental. So what happens when you discover that it has been damaged by a guest? Here's how you can protect yourself from financial losses when it comes to accidents in your rental space.

The Remedy

Make sure you take photos and get invoices for repairs if your property is damaged. For bookings through BDC, send photos to the following email address: [their ten-digit reservation number]@my.booking.com. (e.g., 1266751615@my.booking.com). This sends your photos straight into the guest's reservation, where Booking.com can view the photos and match them directly to your guest. This information will stay on file, assuming that the guest in question continues to use the same email address that they registered with. You won't be able to view this information, and neither will the guest. Booking.com will review your photos, invoices, and other documents, and they will register a guest misconduct note against the guest's account. After filing a complaint, you're not obligated to accept this guest again.

You should also get your own payment processor and collect security deposits. If you don't have a card processing facility, you may lose money if a guest trashes the place. Note that bookings from Airbnb require mediation in the Resolution Centre, which means you have far less control over charging the guest for damages and misconduct.

It is good practice to keep spares of things like remote controls, television sets, and everything else in between. Believe it or not, some guests will steal these items. If you are dealing with damage or theft from an Airbnb reservation, luckily for you, there is host damage protection in place in the form of AirCover. Within 14 days of the responsible guest's checkout, file an AirCover request through their Resolution Centre. After you submit your AirCover request, your guest will have 72 hours to pay. If they decline to pay the full amount or don't respond, you'll be prompted to involve Airbnb support.

There are other alternatives available to hosts for collecting security deposits. I use SUPERHOG, which is a digital trust platform that enables hosts, operators, and guests to confidently transact in the short-term rental space. All the properties that I manage are protected through them, and they contact my guests directly to complete their booking validation (including ID verification).

9. PARTIES, PROSTITUTION, BROTHELS, AND LAST-MINUTE BOOKINGS

The Wart

These guests are arguably some of the worst you'll ever encounter. Even if they're willing to pay, guests that host loud parties and pop-up brothels are bad for business. The loud noise and the flow of punters will annoy your neighbours, which can result in a host of other issues.

I've experienced guests who've booked my property to throw a party and have completely trashed the place. It's safe to say I'm completely fed up with dealing with these types of guests. Although, until recently, this hadn't happened to me for two and a half years.

The Remedy

If you suspect that your guests are planning a party or are prostitutes, make sure you run the mobile number they gave you on Google and TrueCaller. It's also in your best interest to install CCTV or a Ring security doorbell system so you can keep track of people coming in and out of the apartment (note that it will only take footage of the outside, never the inside as this violates privacy).

Take extra precautions when vetting guests and always trust your gut. Look for red flags when guests make last-minute bookings. For example, are they booking from a local address? Do they seem too eager to get the check-in details? Has their card been declined, leaving you unable to collect payments? These scenarios indicate that something isn't quite right with this booking, and you should anticipate trouble ahead.

You will need to vet your guests thoroughly. Make sure they know that the area is regularly monitored and under surveillance both for their safety and to ward off troublesome guests. A guest planning a party or a pop-up brothel may think twice before booking your accommodation. You can add a clause similar to the following in your booking terms or OTA listing:

> *The apartment has its own private entrance, although the entrances to all other properties are covered by CCTV and monitored for the safety of our guests and to ensure only the number of guests that checked in are staying at the property.*

Asking the lead guest for a list of people who will be at the apartment and avoiding bookings from your local area without a valid reason are also key to preventing suspicious last-minute bookings from turning into something worse. You may lose revenue, but it'll keep you sane and in the game longer. Here are more tips for avoiding shady bookings:

- Don't accept last-minute bookings that you are uncomfortable with. If it feels dodgy, it usually is. Most of the issues I've encountered came from last-minute bookings. I now block an evening, even if it's still available, especially on Fridays and Saturdays. This prevents people from being able to book the apartment at the last minute.

- Make sure the minimum age of your lead guest is at least 24.

- Request government-issued photo ID. This usually comes in the form of a driving licence, which allows you to check their address.

- The guest must submit their address, including their postcode.

- Search the guest's name on Facebook and Google to verify if they exist. If there's no profile on Facebook or no such name on Google, take caution!

- As will be covered in Chapter 3, make sure you get a picture of the guest's card that shows the name and the last four digits. This will also be helpful in the event of a chargeback and will also ensure that the card isn't stolen.

- This piece of advice might not be too helpful for BDC, but for Airbnb, you should check how long the guest has had a profile and how many reviews they have.

- Look out for common guest behaviour patterns. The worst guests are usually terribly enthusiastic about obtaining their check-in details prior to even having their booking validated. They usually want to know everything about gaining access to the accommodation, and this is generally followed up by countless erratic phone calls. This should set alarm bells ringing!

- My ultimate rule is that if there's any doubt, there should be no doubt! Always follow your gut instinct and try to ensure that your calendar is booked in advance to avoid dealing with last-minute chancers.

- Should you manage to allow a dodgy booking to slip through the net, consider using a local security company to check your apartment every hour. I've done this by paying a local security company £15 per hour, which I especially recommend if there are concerts and events in the area. I also tell guests that security will be on patrol, and that if they are partying or making noise at unacceptable levels, they will be asked to leave or be removed from the premises. The security call-out fee will also be deducted from their deposit. It seems harsh, but it's gotten rid of most of the complaints from neighbours.

10. SMOKING GUESTS

The Wart

Some guests have no regard for your property and may still smoke indoors, despite your strict no smoking policy. Unfortunately, no matter what sign you post in relation to non-smoking rooms, there are some guests who just don't care, and if they need to smoke, they will. You'll end up with carpet burns, a smelly property, and questions about how to bill them for it. This is very frustrating and results in increased cleaning costs; not to mention, it's not very pleasant for the new guests checking in the same day! So how do you deal with this?

The Remedy

First, make sure you collect a security deposit. You should also consider altering your booking terms to highlight that guests will be charged a hefty smoking fee for cleaning and deodorising the apartment. Mention that you'll also charge them for every day that you're unable to rent out the property due to the smell of smoke. Investing in an ozone generator machine from Amazon to switch on between changeovers will help eliminate any smoking smells. It's not ideal if you have back-to-back bookings, but if you have a few hours free before the next guest arrives, then it's a great solution for you.

You can use the following clause in your booking T&Cs:

Smoking is strictly forbidden in the accommodation. Should we find any evidence of smoking in the room, you will be liable to pay a smoking penalty and may also incur the cost for every day that we're unable to rent out the property while cleaning and deodorising the apartment.

CHAPTER THREE
PAYMENT AND LEGAL ISSUES

11. CHARGEBACKS, DISPUTED PAYMENTS, AND STOLEN CARDS

The Wart

A guest has booked your accommodation, paid, stayed, and left the premises. Everyone is happy, and all is well, right? Until you suddenly get a notification from your payment merchant saying that your guest has made a payment dispute against you, resulting in funds being withdrawn from your bank account. It's an upsetting scenario that has happened to me one too many times while managing properties and is likely to happen to you too.

Chargebacks result in the following unfavourable scenarios:

- A loss of time and money while trying to sort out the payment dispute
- Hours spent staring at photos of cards as you try to determine whether the card they used was photoshopped
- Having to do the admin yourself because outsourcing means they won't check the signatures,

driver's licences, passports, addresses, and cards as carefully as you

- Endless worries about guests using stolen cards and potentially damaging your property

Stolen Cards

Cards that have been stolen have a lifespan of approximately six days before banks automatically stop them. Because of this, criminals usually book, stay, and leave within six days, which is what makes last-minute bookings high risk (although last-minute bookings will account for about 50% of your total bookings). Knowing how to avoid stolen cards will prevent chargebacks on your account and will also allow you to reap the benefits of last-minute bookings without the risk.

Here's what fraudsters usually do with stolen cards at serviced accommodation:

- They buy stolen card numbers from the dark web and spend as much money as possible before the card is stopped.

- They collect numbers using hardware that copies the card details of people around them.
- They rent apartments and 'sell' them to someone else for underage sex parties.
- They hold their own underage sex parties in apartments and charge men to attend.
- They rent an apartment, advertise it on Gumtree as a long-term rental, and collect a deposit plus the first month's rent.
- They damage apartments because they aren't using their own hard-earned money and their intention is to create a payment dispute.

The scenarios listed above set your serviced accommodation business back. Every chargeback you receive costs £15 if you're using Stripe as a payment processor, and you'll also lose more revenue by having to spend time collecting evidence to ensure the dispute is ruled in your favour.

The Remedy
The Importance of T&Cs, Photo ID, and Proof of Card

The best solution to chargebacks, disputed payments, and stolen cards is to establish solid terms and conditions between you and your guests. There is an array of free and paid templates available online that you can tweak to your liking. The lead booker (the cardholder) should sign the terms and conditions and send photo identification like a driver's licence, passport, or ID card. Proof of their payment card is also key to preventing any issues.

If you happen to be doing remote self-check-ins and aren't meeting your guests, requesting a photo of the front of the credit card that's being used to make the booking will suffice. Make sure that it shows the last four digits of the card number and the cardholder's name. Here's a general idea of what you can say to your guests to ensure they provide proof of payment:

Please note that proof of payment card is required and must be shown electronically prior to checking in to your accommodation.

We require a photo of the front of the credit card used to make the booking. Please conceal your credit card number, ensuring only the last four digits and the name on the front of the card are shown.

The above will allow you to match the name on the card to the person booking and the person signing the terms and conditions. I personally only accept signed terms and conditions and photo ID from the authorised cardholder. In most cases, if the card has been stolen, the person booking will be reluctant to send you copies that prove that they're the authorised cardholder.

Using an e-signing platform like RightSignature or Signable will simplify this process for you. It allows you to upload the booking terms as a document, add or create text, dates, checkboxes, and signature fields. You can also add attachments, a feature I use at the bottom of the document to prompt guests to upload important information like their photo ID and proof of payment card.

Securing Transactions for Your Guests

Strong consumer authentication (SCA) is a required feature that came into force on 14 September 2019, consisting of new authentication requirements for online payments made in Europe. This is a part of the Revised Payment Services Directive (PSD2). This was introduced to protect customers who make purchases online. Businesses that use European Stripe accounts are required to update their Stripe integration to make sure that they support the new SCA requirements, which will change how your customers authenticate their online payments. To meet SCA requirements, card payments need an alternative user experience such as 3D Secure. If they don't meet these basic requirements, your customers' banks may decline the transaction.

Chargebacks related to fraudulent activity and stolen cards require you to use a secure payment processor to verify and validate the authenticity of the card user. Stripe Radar is a technology that can check postal and ZIP codes and match them with the country of origin of the card user. Another option is Worldpay's 3D Secure 'Pay by Link', which allows you to send invoices for deposits or reservations. The guest can pay the invoice, but as the cardholder, they'll need to know the passcode on their account. This is the 3D verification element that requires the cardholder's bank to authenticate the transaction. This is the equivalent of a card chip and PIN machine. No PIN equals no transaction, and if someone gets hold of a guest's PIN, the guest is at fault, not the merchant. This means no more stolen cards or charge-backs!

An invoice could potentially sit in the guest's inbox and not be paid, but according to BDC, if your fine print states that payment is required prior to the guest's arrival (at least 24 hours before the check-in date), then you're allowed to cancel the reservation without any penalties. After all, the guest hasn't adhered to the booking conditions. This also applies if a declined card isn't updated in a timely manner.

Challenging Chargebacks and Payment Disputes

When a chargeback or dispute occurs, you have to prove that the card user stayed at your accommodation or at least booked and paid for said accommodation. The next step is to ensure that you record and document the communication between you and the guest, in case they say something that proves they did stay at your accommodation. I usually keep texts and emails from the guests, notifications from KeyNest that state that keys were collected by the guest, and messages from my answering service (answer.co.uk) as evidence.

Winning a dispute requires you to be sure of who made the payment for your accommodation. If you can't meet your guests physically and also aren't doing all the above, then how can you be sure of where the payment comes from, and how would you prove this? Keep in mind that you can't win a chargeback case using CCTV footage, so make sure all your bookings are well documented.

If the reservation was made on Booking.com, you'll be able to download a document in your extranet called the 'Chargeback Defence Document'. This handy document includes all the evidence you need to submit to the merchant's bank. All you have to do is go to Reservations, input the date of the reservation to find your guest, and browse the relevant documents.

There may be rare instances where payment disputes against you pertain to delivering 'an unacceptable product' and not fraudulent activity. The dispute process for this remains the same, except you'll have to display the condition of the property as well as how you did your best to address the guest's concerns and complaints. I've experienced this myself when a guest disputed a £5k payment. I won the dispute because I was able to provide photos of the property and emails between the guest and me.

It's important to note that these are merely preventative measures and don't guarantee that your guests won't file any chargebacks. If all of this sounds like too much for you, it's best to stick to having the OTAs manage your payments. It's one of the best ways to prevent chargebacks because that third party is then liable for any disputes.

Ring-Fencing Funds Using Secondary Holding Accounts
Having a secondary holding account that's connected to your payment processor can reduce the negative effects of chargebacks. This is because it'll allow you to

take out as much money as possible and put it into your bank account, which will remain unaffected by disputes.

12. DISPUTE WITH YOUR LANDLORD, AGENT, DEVELOPER, OR NEIGHBOUR

The Wart

Disputes can arise with the landlord, agent, or developer. You may receive an email from the agent citing reports from the management company that you're advertising the apartment on Airbnb and other sites, which is in breach of the lease. They may state that the apartment can be used for serviced accommodation but only for long-term stays.

What if your neighbours are anti-short-let stays? This will definitely affect your serviced accommodation business. If you've just started operating, you may be confused about what to do in these situations. But before you give up the apartment and lose your financial investment, read through the next section for potential remedies.

The Remedy

First, ask yourself: is what the estate agent is offering an appropriate apartment for your business? Were you up-front about operating short-term stays in the apartment? Did the owner know what you were planning? Does your tenancy agreement explicitly state that you're permitted to operate serviced accommodation? If the answers to these questions are 'no', then you may be in a typical situation where the estate agent was eager to get the deal, regardless of whether the owner was aware of the implications. Now that the management is involved, they want to evade accountability for allowing short-term stays at the apartment.

One practical solution is to have a booking window and block out your diary to only allow bookings up to a certain number of months in the future. Having a watertight agreement drawn up also helps. You'll have to consult with a qualified legal professional for this. You should also be prepared to go to court if things go left.

You should also verify neighbour complaints by installing Wi-Fi-based noise monitors that record decibel levels.

The Minut device is a great option. It's also in your best interest to have good relationships with your neighbours and ensure they know your complaint policy. Try to work with them and offer them your contact details to reassure them that you're available to deal with any misconduct and disruption from guests.

If you receive a noise complaint from a neighbour, it's best to call the guest, let them know that there's been a complaint, and then ask them to keep the noise down. After that, give the guest 10 minutes to stop the noise. Should the noise not stop, you'll most likely get another call from the neighbour, at which point you should attend and observe. If the guests are hosting a party or are too loud, it's best to consider a riot act or throwing them out. It's important to charge for your time should you be called out to settle a noise dispute. Make sure you stipulate that there will be a £100 charge to their card in your T&Cs.

Keep in mind that you could be the most considerate serviced accommodation host, and your neighbour could simply hate what you're doing because they don't want to live near a 'hotel'. This will most likely lead to frequent complaints.

The Legalities of Serviced Accommodation

Depending on how the agreement is drafted, a short-term let can be legally valid. However, you likely don't have the legal protection that a personal AST offers. You may use your contract as evidence of permission to short-term let, but it might not contain permission from the management or freeholder.

To handle a dispute, you should explain the agreement you have in place. Information like how long you have left on the lease/agreement, what the value of your bookings is, and whether you're offering 1-to-14-day stays is important. You should also ask the agent to provide evidence that they've obtained permission for you to run a serviced accommodation in the unit(s). You may have to leave and find another unit if this issue becomes legal.

When it comes to chain agents, the usual issue is that the person working at the branch gets paid commission, and the short-term lets have to use either the AST or the company let agreement, which is mandated by head-quarters. This results in a 'written by layman' clause being inserted, which may not pass HQ's scrutiny. The agreement should be clear and robust as this will cover you if things go awry. Remember that the lease trumps whatever contract you have and will determine whether you can operate or not, but the contract will determine what costs you face to exit early or what possible redress you have against the agent or landlord (e.g., for your relocation costs).

13. PAYMENT MERCHANT LOCKOUTS

The Wart

The benefit of using a card processing facility is that you'll be able to charge guests for damage they've caused, and you'll also be able to take direct bookings without paying commission to booking sites like BDC and Airbnb. Doing this also allows you to take non-refundable bookings and get the money immediately.

A downside of using a card processing facility is that you have to pay for it, and you may unknowingly take payments from stolen cards if you don't put systems in place to prevent this. I wouldn't be able to sleep peacefully knowing that a guest could trash my apartment and disappear, leaving me to foot the bill. The ability to go back and charge a guest's payment card is sometimes the only security we have as hosts.

Your payment merchant can freeze funds or suspend your account without any warning or due process. I've heard a few horror stories about Stripe doing this to hosts. If you dig into the terms and conditions a little closer, you'll see that Stripe reserves the right to suspend or freeze your account whenever they want. Regardless of whether you're a high-risk merchant, this is a frightening clause. The last thing you want to do is build a business on borrowed time. Even worse, Stripe could 'Match-List' your business. Member Alert to Control High-Risk (MATCH) is a credit risk review system that banks consult before considering issuing a merchant account. The issue with being on the list? You're effectively blackballed as a company. You cannot process credit cards. Even additional payment methods are challenging to come by.

The Remedy

Your recourse against suspended accounts is to keep a watchful eye on the chargebacks attributed to your Stripe account. So what is an acceptable level of chargeback transactions? Well, ideally, none. But obviously, that's not realistic. If you're over a 0.5% chargeback ratio, you should be very worried indeed. That meets the criteria they set in their terms and conditions to shut your account down within 24 hours, hold payouts destined for your bank account, and eliminate your cash flow.

I would also recommend having more than one payment merchant account. A backup account is crucial in this line of work. If you prefer convenience and efficiency like me, you can also opt for a managing agent model approach that uses several client accounts. You may consider using a separate merchant account for every property or client. I use Stripe and have individual bank accounts for each landlord, which are linked to their own designated Stripe accounts. Should an account be frozen or suspended, I've minimised my exposure to risk because the other accounts will remain unaffected. Do do this yourself; you'll need a channel manager with the ability to link individual Stripe accounts to various properties using different payment routes.

There are also payment processors that can provide specialist high-risk merchant accounts with higher built-in risk tolerances. They understand that chargebacks, refunds, and the occasional instance of fraud will happen, and a good payment processor will help you mitigate the damage those unfortunate events do to your processing. It is good business practice to divert a portion of your sales to a specialised high-risk merchant account (known as load balancing) to build up a solid processing history alongside your Stripe card transactions. This way, if the inevitable happens over at Stripe, you have a back-up plan in place.

14. THE 90-DAY RULE

The Wart

If you're operating in London, it's important for you to be aware of the 90-day limit so you can be compliant. The 90-day rule states that hosts are unable to let out entire homes for more than 90 days per calendar year. Your stays of 90 days or less cannot, when added together, total more than 90 days in any one calendar year. If they do, then you need planning permission. Though you can't legally circumvent the 90-day rule, you can maximise revenue by diversifying your letting types.

The Remedy

Optimise the letting cycle by using a combination of long-term, short-term, and holiday lets. This includes holiday lets on Airbnb, Expedia, and Booking.com during the peak season to maximise your earning potential. Combine this with long-term stays on Zoopla or Rightmove for an extended period during off-peak seasons, or corporate bookings for short-to-mid-term stays. You can negotiate your rates based on bookings with a minimum stay of three months.

Make sure you build relationships with your existing guests as these can be potentially converted into long-term bookings. Websites like Homelike are also great for longer stays. You can also contact insurance companies that need help with relocation claims and use LinkedIn to contact HR managers that need accommodation for their employees. Try researching large construction projects close to your accommodation to help with this.

SUMMING UP

R unning a serviced accommodation business presents a great opportunity to invest in property and receive revenue, but it's imperative that you do your due diligence and research beforehand. I hope that this book, filled with advice from experts and a myriad of my experiences, inspires you to overcome the common pitfalls of serviced accommodation and guides you on your path to success. I would like to thank you for choosing this book and trusting me to share my insights with you. I am grateful.

Of course, I invite you to connect with me on social media! @RaeAnneRainford is where I can usually be found on one of your favourites: either Facebook, Instagram, LinkedIn or TikTok! But if you're really wanting to kickstart your journey to success in serviced accommodation then I encourage you to join The Short Let Collaborative Facebook group. Support and connect with other members who want to up-level rental income and unlock their property's true potential through Airbnb and short lets.

BONUS - MY TOP TEN TIPS FOR NEW OPERATORS

1. Start with Shorter Stays

Shorter stays have a more rigorous turnover, but they help with reviews and making sure your place isn't damaged. They'll also allow you to get more practice and flex your 'hosting muscles'.

As previously mentioned in another section, some guests deliberately target new listings and cause damage purely because you have little to no experience. It's better to have guests like this in and out than spend months in dispute. Also, be mindful of landlord/tenant laws in your area that may kick in for stays over a certain period of time.

2. Check the Space Between Each Guest, Even If You Have a Cleaning Service

This is imperative when you start hosting. It will not only help give you peace of mind, but it will also give you insight into the types of habits and norms that people generally have. It'll give you a baseline to know if things are amiss in the future.

3. Make Your Decisions Upfront

Decide early if you're open to hosting pets, children, or families and stick to that decision. You can change your rules as time passes, but it's key to be clear about your expectations from the beginning. Don't make any exceptions to get bookings, even if it is tempting. Wait until you've hosted several stays to evaluate whether you're ready to change your policies.

4. Leave House Rules in Multiple Places

Make sure you post your house rules in your listing. You can also leave copies in a house guide and explain them in person to the guest if possible. In my experience, most guests need at least three opportunities to read and thoroughly understand the rules. The vast majority do not read them on Airbnb and other OTAs.

5. Be Careful About the Capacity of Your Listing, Especially Early in Hosting

It can be quite tempting to allow more guests than you would like, to get more money, but I would advise against this. Don't give the impression that your space holds more people than listed by mentioning things like air mattresses and sofas unless you want guests using them to try and bring extra people. This is because many guests don't count their kids, friends, or grandkids as extra people and will often try to get away with bringing more people to the space than they have booked.

After you get a booking, make sure you verify guest counts the day you send check-in instructions. Don't allow any parties and remember that extra guests equal extra cleaning, more wear and tear, more towels, and more showers, which is a disturbance if you homeshare.

6. Always Be As Polite and Kind As Possible, Even When People Are Difficult

Remain professional regardless of guest behaviour but be firm and stick to the rules about your space. Don't be afraid to say, 'I am sorry; this doesn't seem to be working out. Let me call Airbnb and see if they can connect you with a more suitable stay,' if you need to.

7. Leave Fair Reviews

I recently received an inquiry from a guest with a three-star rating in one category but glowing reviews from five hosts. How does this happen? You can always ask for help with wording your review, but you need to be honest and mention if there was an issue. It can be a real hurdle to a new host who is looking to build up their own reviews, but honesty is very important.

8. Understand That Your Space Needs to Be Cleaner Than the Average Home

I have a cleaning service that cleans my primary house, but their work would not meet Airbnb's standards. In my own space, I make sure I clean for an extra hour or so each time to make sure she didn't miss a spot. My home isn't as spotless as my Airbnb, but no one can say that my home is dirty. It's just a different level of cleanliness.

9. Watch Your Payouts

Airbnb has bugs from time to time, which may cause payout issues. It takes persistence to resolve things if a payout gets missed. I recently went through three months of haggling and over two dozen calls to support to get a payment I was owed.

If a guest alerts you about payment issues or Airbnb cancels the reservation due to payment issues, you'll likely have a hard time collecting money from the stay. Keep that in mind if the guest asks to re-book your accommodation.

10. Be Realistic

Not everyone is a serial killer, and not everyone is a saint. Always tread with caution when welcoming guests to your accommodation. Give them the benefit of the doubt and verify important information for your safety.